BETTER TOGETHER

AUTHORS

ELAINE MEI AOKI • VIRGINIA ARNOLD • JAMES FLOOD • JAMES V. HOFFMAN • DIANE LAPP

MIRIAM MARTINEZ • ANNEMARIE SULLIVAN PALINCSAR • MICHAEL PRIESTLEY • CARL B. SMITH

WILLIAM H. TEALE • JOSEFINA VILLAMIL TINAJERO • ARNOLD W. WEBB • KAREN D. WOOD

 **Macmillan McGraw-Hill**

NEW YORK • FARMINGTON

Authors, Consultants, and Reviewers

MULTICULTURAL AND EDUCATIONAL
CONSULTANTS

Alma Flor Ada, Yvonne Beamer, Joyce Buckner,
Helen Gillotte, Cheryl Hudson, Narcita Medina,
Lorraine Monroe, James R. Murphy, Sylvia Peña,
Joseph B. Rubin, Ramon Santiago, Cliff Trafzer,
Hai Tran, Esther Lee Yao

LITERATURE CONSULTANTS

Ashley Bryan, Joan I. Glazer, Paul Janeczko,
Margaret H. Lippert

INTERNATIONAL CONSULTANTS

Edward B. Adams, Barbara Johnson,
Raymond L. Marshall

MUSIC AND AUDIO CONSULTANTS

John Farrell, Marilyn C. Davidson,
Vincent Lawrence, Sarah Pirtle, Susan R. Synder,
Rick and Deborah Witkowski, Eastern Sky Media
Services, Inc.

TEACHER REVIEWERS

Terry Baker, Jane Bauer, James Bedi, Nora Bickel,
Vernell Bowen, Donald Cason, Jean Chaney,
Carolyn Clark, Alan Cox, Kathryn DesCarpentrie,
Carol L. Ellis, Roberta Gale, Brenda Huffman,
Erma Inscore, Sharon Kidwell, Elizabeth Love,
Isabel Marcus, Elaine McCraney, Michelle Moraros,
Earlene Parr, Dr. Richard Potts, Jeanette Pulliam,
Michael Rubin, Henrietta Sakamaki,
Kathleen Cultron Sanders, Belinda Snow,
Dr. Jayne Steubing, Margaret Mary Sulentic,
Barbara Tate, Seretta Vincent,
Willard Waite, Barbara Wilson, Veronica York

Macmillan/McGraw-Hill

*A Division of The **McGraw·Hill** Companies*

Copyright © 1997 Macmillan/McGraw-Hill,
a Division of the Educational and Professional
Publishing Group of The McGraw-Hill Companies, Inc.

Macmillan/McGraw-Hill
1221 Avenue of the Americas
New York, New York 10020
Printed in the United States of America

ISBN 0-02-181125-3 / 2, L.6, U.3
1 2 3 4 5 6 7 8 9 WEB 02 01 00 99 98 97 96

Better Together

Contents

The MYSTERIOUS Tadpole

by Steven Kellogg

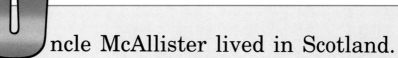

Uncle McAllister lived in Scotland.

Every year he sent Louis a birthday gift for his nature collection.

"This is the best one yet!" cried Louis.

The next day he took his entire collection to school for show-and-tell.

"Class, this is a tadpole," said Mrs. Shelbert. She asked Louis to bring it back often so they could all watch it become a frog.

239

Louis named the tadpole Alphonse. Every day Alphonse ate several cheeseburgers.

Louis found that he was eager to learn.

When Alphonse became too big for his jar, Louis moved him to the sink.

After Alphonse outgrew the sink, Louis's parents agreed to let him use the bathtub.

242

One day Mrs. Shelbert decided that Alphonse was not turning into an ordinary frog.

She asked Louis to stop bringing him to school.

By the time summer vacation arrived, Alphonse was enormous.

"He's too big for the bathtub," said Louis's mother.

"He's too big for the apartment," said Louis's father.

"He needs a swimming pool," said Louis.

"There is no place in our apartment for a swimming pool," said his parents.

Louis suggested that they buy the parking lot next door and build a swimming pool.

"It would cost more money than we have," said his parents. "Your tadpole will have to be donated to the zoo."

The thought of Alphonse in a cage made Louis very sad.

hen, in the middle of the night, Louis remembered that the junior high had a swimming pool that nobody used during the summer.

Louis hid Alphonse under a rug and smuggled him into the school.

After making sure that Alphonse felt at home, Louis went back to bed.

Every morning Louis spent several hours swimming with his friend. In the afternoon he earned the money for Alphonse's cheeseburgers by delivering newspapers.

Meanwhile the training continued.
Alphonse learned to retrieve things from the
bottom of the pool.

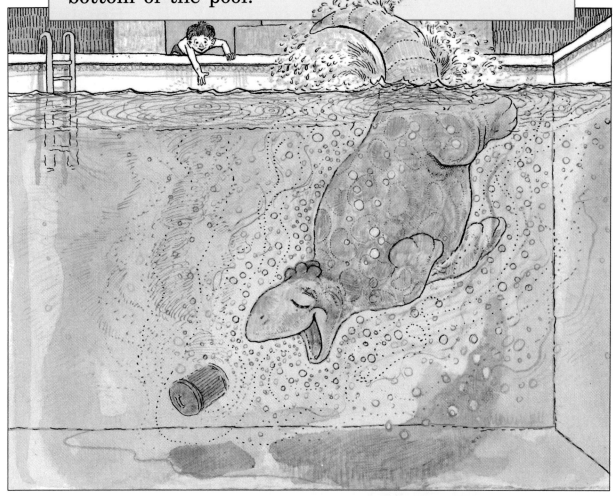

ummer vacation passed quickly. Louis worried what would happen to Alphonse now that school had reopened.

As soon as the first day ended, he ran to the junior high. The students were getting ready for after-school activities.

Louis arrived just as the first swimming race began.

Alphonse was delighted to see all the swimmers.

"It's a submarine from another planet!" bellowed the coach. "Call the police! Call the Navy!"

"No! It's a tadpole!" cried Louis. "He's my pet!"

The coach was upset and confused.

"You have until tomorrow," he cried, "to get that creature out of the pool!"

Louis didn't know what to do. On the way home he met his friend Miss Seevers, the librarian, and he told her his problem.

Miss Seevers went back to the junior high school with Louis, but when she saw Alphonse, she was so shocked that she dropped her purse and the books she was carrying into the swimming pool. Alphonse retrieved them.

Then Miss Seevers telephoned Louis's Uncle McAllister in Scotland. He told her that he had caught the little tadpole in Loch Ness, a large lake near his cottage.

Miss Seevers said, "I'm convinced that your uncle has given you a very rare Loch Ness monster!"

"I don't care!" cried Louis. "He's my pet, and I love him!" He begged Miss Seevers to help him raise enough money to buy the parking lot near his apartment so he could build a swimming pool for Alphonse.

Suddenly Miss Seevers had an idea.

"In 1639 there was a battle in our city's harbor," she said. "A pirate treasure ship was sunk, and no one has ever been able to find it. But perhaps we can!"

256

The next morning Miss Seevers and Louis rented a boat.

In the middle of the harbor Louis showed Alphonse a picture of a treasure chest.

Alphonse disappeared under the water.

Louis and Miss Seevers bought the parking lot.

They hired some helpers.

And when the pool was completed, all

the children in the city were invited to swim.

261

That night Louis said, "Alphonse, next week is my birthday, which means that we've been friends for almost a year."

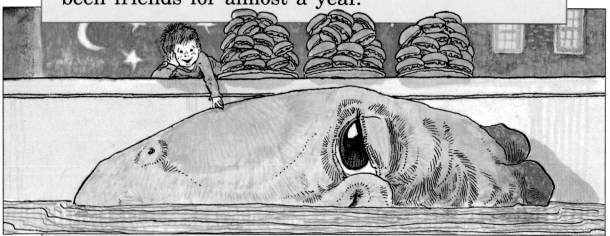

Far away in Scotland Uncle McAllister was also thinking about the approaching birthday. While out hiking he discovered an unusual stone in a clump of grass and sticks.

"A perfect gift for my nephew!" he cried.

"I'll deliver it in person!"

Uncle McAllister arrived at Louis's apartment and gave Louis the present.

Louis couldn't wait to add it to his collection.

Suddenly a crack appeared in the stone. . . .

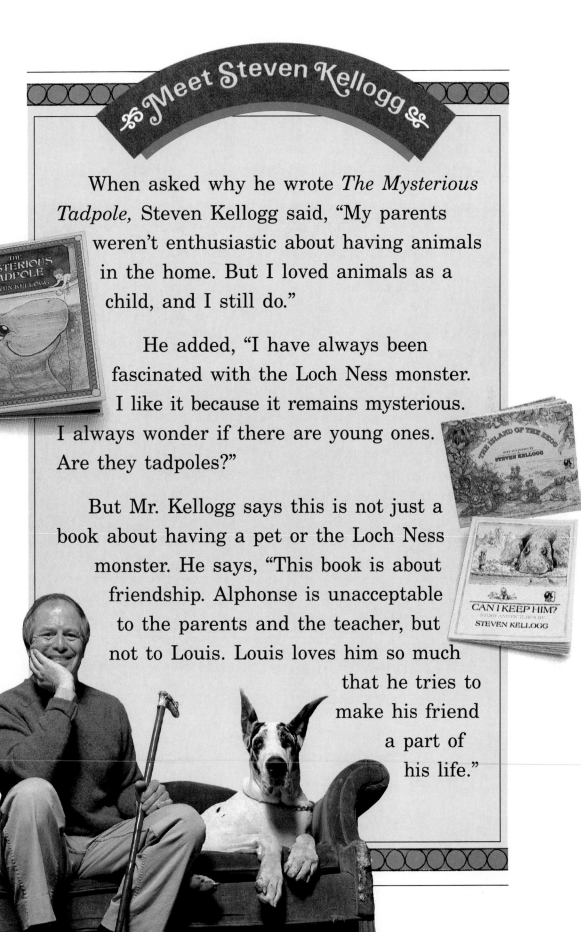

Meet Steven Kellogg

When asked why he wrote *The Mysterious Tadpole,* Steven Kellogg said, "My parents weren't enthusiastic about having animals in the home. But I loved animals as a child, and I still do."

He added, "I have always been fascinated with the Loch Ness monster. I like it because it remains mysterious. I always wonder if there are young ones. Are they tadpoles?"

But Mr. Kellogg says this is not just a book about having a pet or the Loch Ness monster. He says, "This book is about friendship. Alphonse is unacceptable to the parents and the teacher, but not to Louis. Louis loves him so much that he tries to make his friend a part of his life."

PUPPY AND I

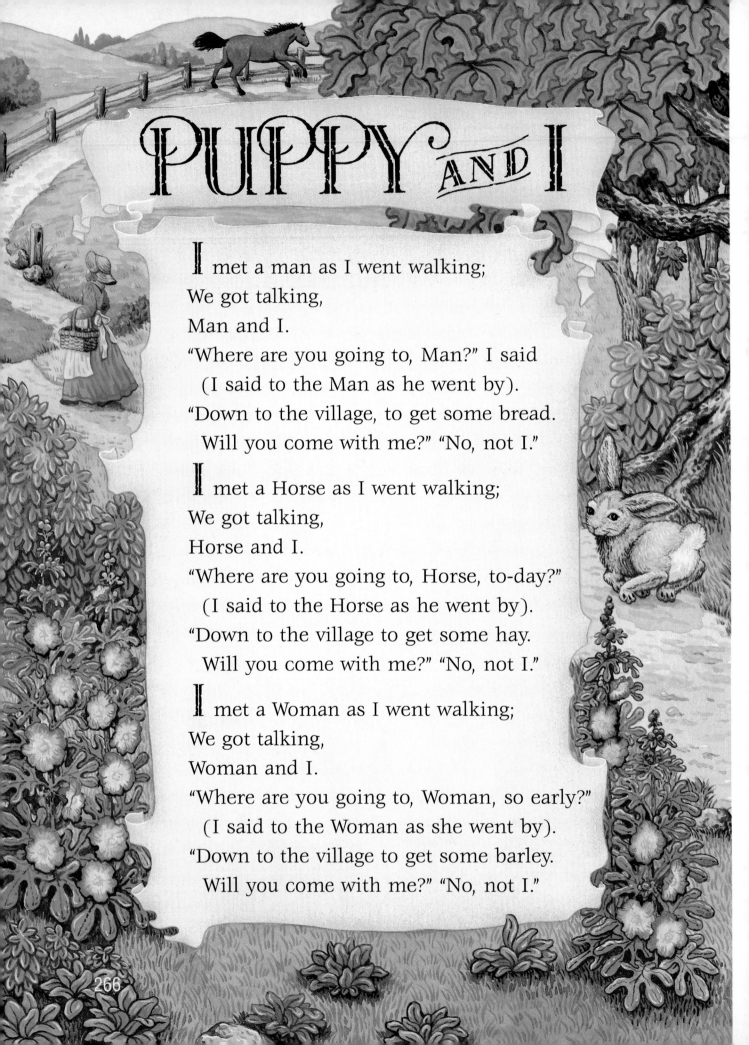

I met a man as I went walking;
We got talking,
Man and I.
"Where are you going to, Man?" I said
  (I said to the Man as he went by).
"Down to the village, to get some bread.
  Will you come with me?" "No, not I."

I met a Horse as I went walking;
We got talking,
Horse and I.
"Where are you going to, Horse, to-day?"
  (I said to the Horse as he went by).
"Down to the village to get some hay.
  Will you come with me?" "No, not I."

I met a Woman as I went walking;
We got talking,
Woman and I.
"Where are you going to, Woman, so early?"
  (I said to the Woman as she went by).
"Down to the village to get some barley.
  Will you come with me?" "No, not I."

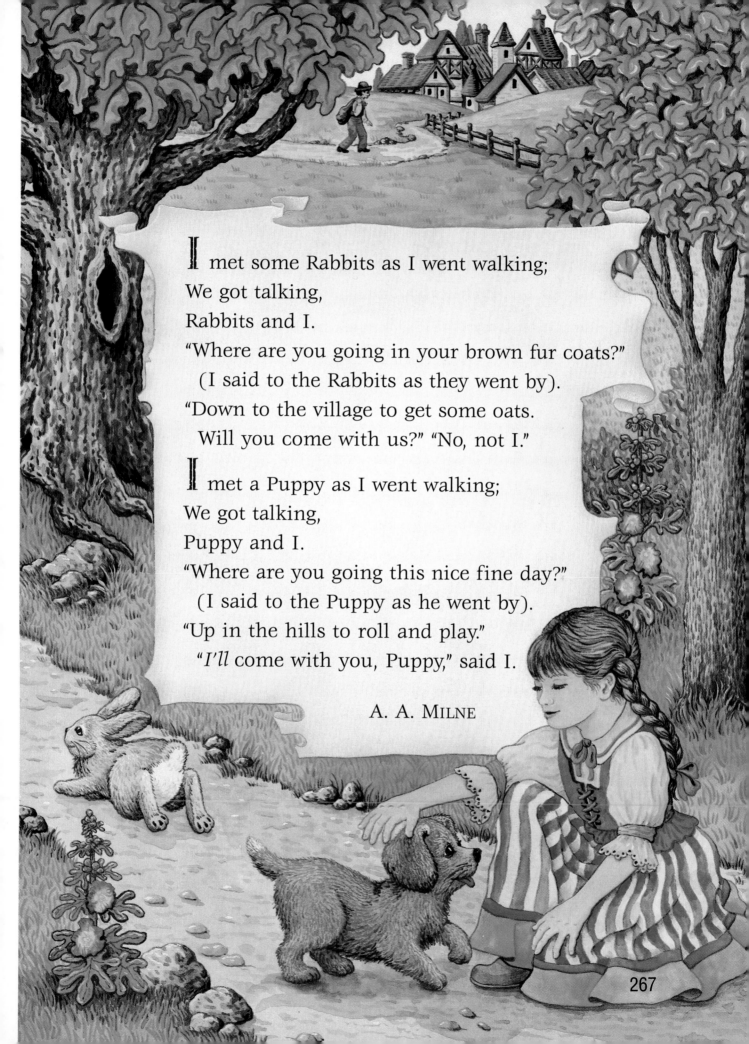

I met some Rabbits as I went walking;
We got talking,
Rabbits and I.
"Where are you going in your brown fur coats?"
  (I said to the Rabbits as they went by).
"Down to the village to get some oats.
  Will you come with us?" "No, not I."

I met a Puppy as I went walking;
We got talking,
Puppy and I.
"Where are you going this nice fine day?"
  (I said to the Puppy as he went by).
"Up in the hills to roll and play."
  "*I'll* come with you, Puppy," said I.

A. A. MILNE

267

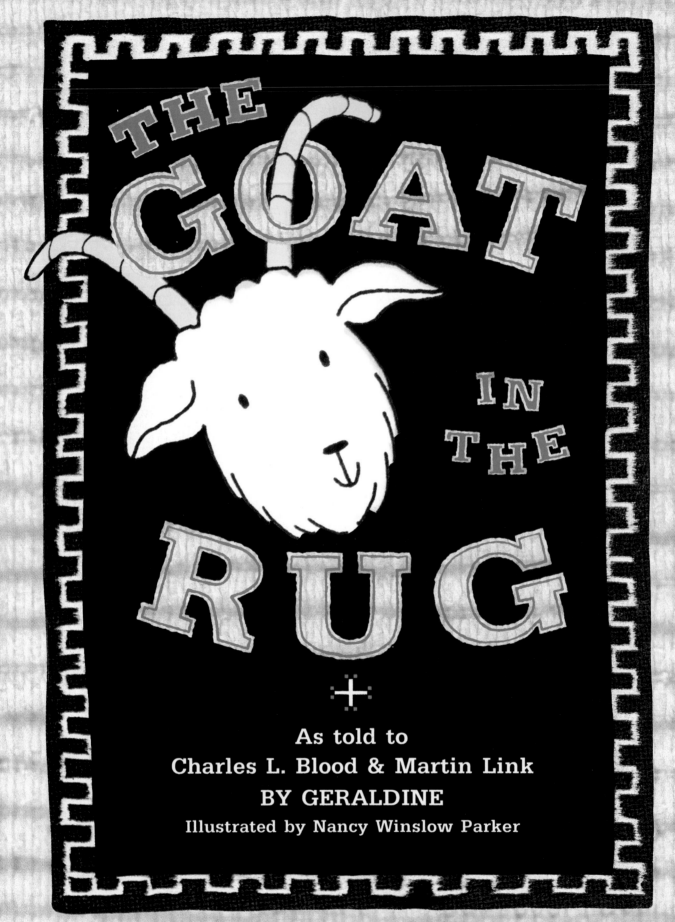

THE GOAT IN THE RUG

As told to
Charles L. Blood & Martin Link
BY GERALDINE
Illustrated by Nancy Winslow Parker

My name is Geraldine and I live near a place called Window Rock with my Navajo friend, Glenmae. It's called Window Rock because it has a big round hole in it that looks like a window open to the sky.

Glenmae is called Glenmae most of the time because it's easier to say than her Indian name: Glee 'Nasbah. In English that means something like female warrior, but she's really a Navajo weaver. I guess that's why, one day, she decided to weave me into a rug.

I remember it was a warm, sunny afternoon. Glenmae had spent most of the morning sharpening a large pair of scissors. I had no idea what she was going to use them for, but it didn't take me long to find out.

Before I knew what was happening, I was on the ground and Glenmae was clipping off my wool in great long strands. (It's called mohair, really.) It didn't hurt at all, but I admit I kicked up my heels some. I'm very ticklish for a goat.

I might have looked a little naked and silly afterwards, but my, did I feel nice and cool! So I decided to stick around and see what would happen next.

The first thing Glenmae did was chop up roots from a yucca plant. The roots made a soapy, rich lather when she mixed them with water.

She washed my wool in the suds until it was clean and white.

After that, a little bit of me (you might say) was hung up in the sun to dry. When my wool was dry, Glenmae took out two large square combs with many teeth.

By combing my wool between these carding combs, as they're called, she removed any bits of twigs or burrs and straightened out the fibers. She told me it helped make a smoother yarn for spinning.

Then, Glenmae carefully started to spin my wool—one small bundle at a time—into yarn. I was beginning to find out it takes a long while to make a Navajo rug.

Again and again, Glenmae twisted and pulled, twisted and pulled the wool. Then she spun it around a long, thin stick she called a spindle. As she twisted and pulled and spun, the finer, stronger and smoother the yarn became.

A few days later, Glenmae and I went for a walk. She said we were going to find some special plants she would use to make dye.

I didn't know what "dye" meant, but it sounded like a picnic to me. I do love to eat plants. That's what got me into trouble.

rabbitbrush
wild onion
cliffrose
sumac
juniper
walnuts
dock

277

While Glenmae was out looking for more plants, I ate every one she had already collected in her bucket. Delicious!

The next day, Glenmae made me stay home while she walked miles to a store. She said the dye she could buy wasn't the same as the kind she makes from plants, but since I'd made such a pig of myself, it would have to do.

I was really worried that she would still be angry with me when she got back. She wasn't, though, and pretty soon she had three big potfuls of dye boiling over a fire.

Then I saw what Glenmae had meant by dyeing. She dipped my white wool into one pot . . . and it turned pink! She dipped it in again. It turned a darker pink! By the time she'd finished dipping it in and out and hung it up to dry, it was a beautiful deep red.

After that, she dyed some of my wool brown, and some of it black. I couldn't help wondering if those plants I'd eaten would turn all of me the same colors.

While I was worrying about that, Glenmae started to make our rug. She took a ball of yarn and wrapped it around and around two poles. I lost count when she'd reached three hundred wraps. I guess I was too busy thinking about what it would be like to be the only red, white, black and brown goat at Window Rock.

It wasn't long before Glenmae had finished wrapping. Then she hung the poles with the yarn on a big wooden frame. It looked like a picture frame made of logs—she called it a "loom."

After a whole week of getting ready to weave, Glenmae started. She began weaving at the bottom of the loom. Then, one strand of yarn at a time, our rug started growing toward the top.

A few strands of black.

A few of brown.

A few of red.

In and out. Back and forth.

Until, in a few days, the pattern of our rug was clear to see.

Our rug grew very slowly. Just as every
Navajo weaver before her had done for hundreds
and hundreds of years, Glenmae formed a design
that would never be duplicated.

Then, at last, the weaving was finished! But not until I'd checked it quite thoroughly in front . . .

. . . and in back, did I let Glenmae take our rug off the loom.

There was a lot of me in that rug. I wanted it to be perfect. And it was.

287

Since then, my wool has grown almost long enough for Glenmae and me to make another rug. I hope we do very soon. Because, you see, there aren't too many weavers like Glenmae left among the Navajos.

And there's only one goat like me, Geraldine.

Charles L. Blood and Martin Link

The story *The Goat in the Rug* actually happened. Charles Blood, who is part American Indian, went to a Navajo reservation, where he met Martin Link, who works at the Navajo Travel Museum in Window Rock, Arizona. Mr. Link introduced Mr. Blood to Glenmae and Geraldine.

Mr. Blood explains, "Geraldine lived in the zoo and wandered around freely in the museum where Martin worked."

"And Geraldine was friendly and outgoing," adds Mr. Link. "She wore a bell and came in and out of the museum at will. We got nervous about her being inside sometimes, because she would eat the museum booklets. She would eat anything that wasn't nailed down."

Mr. Link says, "The purpose of writing this book was to show the relationship between Native American culture

Mr. Link

Mr. Blood

and the animal world. Native Americans know how to live in harmony and cooperation with the animals. They can teach us how to do this."

"When I first saw *The Goat in the Rug,* I knew I wanted to draw pictures for it," said Nancy Winslow Parker. "I spent a lot of time looking at exhibits in museums to find out about the Navajos. I also read a lot of books about weaving and studied Navajo rugs and clothes. I used what I learned to make the border designs and the clothes Glenmae wears."

The authors also helped Ms. Parker. "Mr. Link and Mr. Blood gave me photographs of a weaver on a Navajo reservation in Window Rock," she explains. "The photographs helped me a lot."

MEET

Nancy Winslow Parker

A Wool Surprise for Kenji

by Sue Katharine Jackson

art by Dora Leder

colored thread

fabric scraps

vat for dying wool

dyed wool

loom

spinning wheel

raw wool

skeins of spun wool

Kenji's grandmother, Mabs, is a weaver. Kenji likes to spend time with Mabs in her studio. On cold days, Mabs lights the wood stove to warm the studio while she and Kenji work together.

Romney sheep

Sometimes Kenji just looks through bags of wool. Some bags have fluffy bunches of natural grays, blacks, browns, and whites. Other bags have wool that has been cleaned, carded, and dyed different colors. Kenji holds the soft clumps to his cheek while Mabs tells him about the animals the wool comes from.

llama

alpaca

collie

knitting machine

carder

Kenji wishes he could try making the big looms *click clack* the way Mabs does. Mabs says, "Please don't play with the loom, Kenji." But she doesn't mind if he pushes the foot pedal that makes the spinning wheel spin. And when she cards wool to comb and clean it, Kenji turns the crank to operate the carder. He likes to help her.

293

One afternoon Mabs and Kenji work on a special
project together. Mabs pulls a bunch of white wool
out of one bag and asks Kenji to choose some
colored pieces from another. Mabs fills a
bucket with soapy, warm water
and pulls two stools up to
the bucket.

Mabs cups the wool tightly in her
hands and dips it into the warm, soapy water.
She squeezes the wool into a round shape and begins patting,
rubbing, pressing, and shaping the wool pieces. She gives Kenji
the wet, heavy ball and shows him how to pat it, turn it, press
it, rub it, and squeeze it. The wet, soft but scratchy wool
tickles Kenji's hands, and he laughs.

Kenji and Mabs take turns dipping the wool into the bucket and then patting, rubbing, and rounding it. Soon the separate wool pieces begin to hold together in a firm shape. Kenji and Mabs keep working.

Finally Mabs tells Kenji that they are done. "We made a felt ball," she says as she hands Kenji the still-warm, heavy, wet ball. "Let's put it in the dryer for a while." They eat lunch while the felt ball dries. When they take the ball out of the dryer, it feels light and strong. The wool pieces cannot be separated. Kenji practices throwing the ball all over Mabs's yard. He is very proud of the felt ball he and Mabs made.

My Horse, Fly Like a Bird

My horse, fly like a bird

To carry me far

From the arrows of my enemies,

And I will tie red ribbons

To your streaming hair.

Virginia Driving Hawk Sneve
adapted from
a Lakota warrior's
song to his horse

This photograph shows part of a beaded bag made by a Cheyenne River Sioux, somewhere between the years 1885 and 1890. The beads are sewn on a hide and show the Miniconjou chief White Swan.

297

HEY, BUG!

Hey, bug, stay!
Don't run away.
I know a game that we can play.

I'll hold my fingers very still
and you can climb a finger-hill.

No, no.
Don't go.

Here's a wall—a tower, too,
a tiny bug town, just for you.
I've a cookie. You have some.
Take this oatmeal cookie crumb.

Hey, bug, stay!
Hey, bug!
Hey!

Lilian Moore

299

HENRY'S

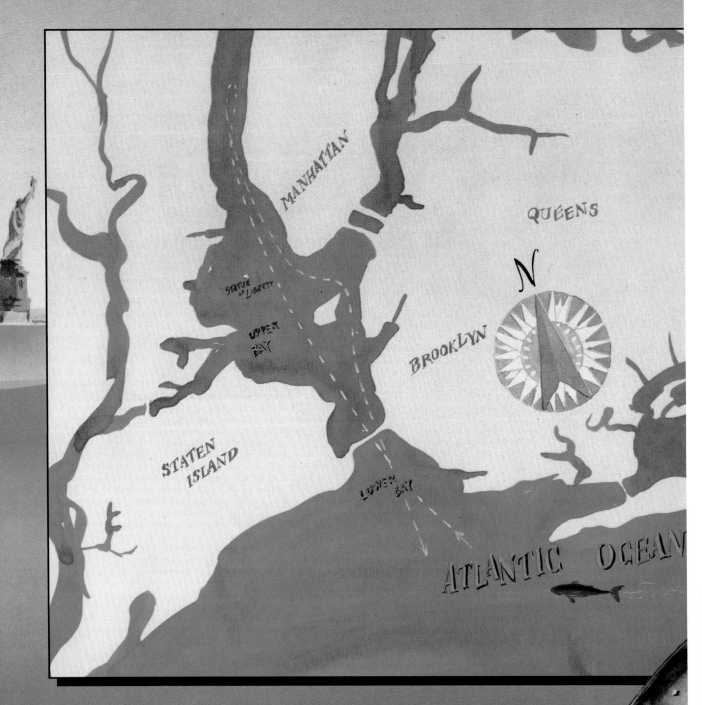

WRONG TURN

WRITTEN BY
HARRIET ZIEFERT

ILLUSTRATED BY
ANDREA BARUFFI

LONG ISLAND

He was a big humpback whale who made a wrong turn. He was swimming in the ocean, and instead of going out to sea, he turned and went up the Hudson River—right into New York Harbor.

No one knew why Henry—for that is what someone named him—wanted to be in New York Harbor. Certainly there was nothing for him to eat in those waters. But there he was.

Henry swam under the Verrazano-Narrows Bridge. The day was bright and sunny, and on the bridge, traffic moved right along. No one up there noticed Henry, but down in the harbor, a tugboat captain did. He signaled to all the other boats: *Watch out for the whale!*

There was lots of excitement. No one could remember seeing a whale in New York Harbor. Everyone was on the lookout for Henry. But where was he?

"Look! There he is!" shouted one of the visitors to the Statue of Liberty. "Take a good look, everyone, because you probably won't see another one like him again."

The *Queen Elizabeth 2* passed
Henry on her way to sea. He was
quite small next to the mighty liner.
The ship sounded its horn and
Henry again dove under the water.

The Coast Guard wanted to help
Henry, so they sent a boat to
follow him.

Henry quickly swam away from the patrol boat. He passed an aircraft carrier, *Intrepid*. Visitors on deck cheered when Henry sent up a magnificent spray.

Suddenly, Henry disappeared.

311

No one saw Henry until evening. By then he was near the World Trade Center. He seemed lost. "We've got to help Henry go back to the ocean," the Coast Guard sailors told each other. "There are too many boats in the harbor. He could get hit!"

313

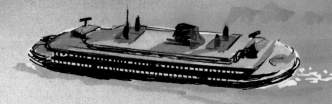

In the twilight, Henry headed past the
Battery into Buttermilk Channel between
Governors Island and Red Hook in Brooklyn.

Two ferries carrying commuters were just leaving their slips. The ferries immediately put their engines in reverse, veered off their courses and . . . avoided a collision with Henry!

Now the Coast Guard was back on Henry's tail. The captain of the cutter was determined to make him turn around and return to the ocean.

And it worked! Perhaps Henry didn't like the noise from the boat's engines. Perhaps he was hungry. For whatever reason, Henry turned around.

Henry swam fast. By the time the moon was in the sky, he was back at the Verrazano-Narrows Bridge, heading out to sea.

Henry left the
harbor, then he dove.
"Good luck, Henry!"

Meet HARRIET ZIEFERT

Harriet Ziefert got the idea for *Henry's Wrong Turn* when she read about Henry, the whale, in the New York newspapers.

Harriet Ziefert decided not to make up what Henry was thinking and feeling. "We don't know why whales sometimes do what Henry did," she says. "We just know that sometimes they get confused."

Ms. Ziefert has written more than a hundred books for children. She tells children, "The more you write, the easier it becomes to write stories."

AND ANDREA BARUFFI

Andrea Baruffi came to the United States from Italy. He says, "*Henry's Wrong Turn* was an exciting book for me because I was painting something that really happened. I live on the Hudson River where the story happened."

For this book, it was important for Mr. Baruffi to show New York Harbor. "One day I took a trip on a boat to see how I should paint the ferries," he says.

WHALE WATCH

Where Do They Go?

A humpback whale that swims in the Pacific Ocean spends its summer off the coast of Alaska. It travels to the waters of Hawaii, a journey of about 3,000 miles (5,556 kilometers), or Mexico, a journey of about 3,381 miles (6,262 kilometers), for the winter.

A humpback whale that swims in the Atlantic Ocean feeds during the summer near Maine, Canada, Greenland, or Iceland. In the winter, it travels to Puerto Rico or the tip of South America, a journey of about 11,433 miles (18,396 kilometers).

Greenland

Iceland

Alaska

Canada

Maine

ATLANTIC OCEAN

North America

Hawaii

Mexico

Puerto Rico

PACIFIC OCEAN

South America

Today, there are about 10,000 humpback whales. A hundred years ago, before hunters killed many of them, there were ten times that number. Now, laws protect humpback whales from hunters.

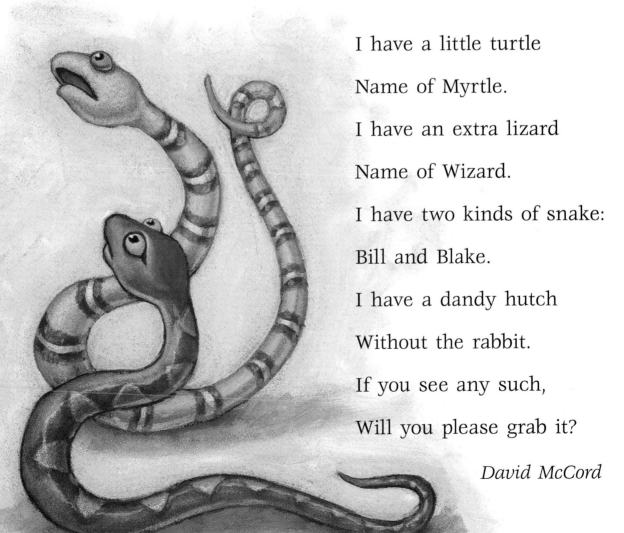

I have a little turtle

Name of Myrtle.

I have an extra lizard

Name of Wizard.

I have two kinds of snake:

Bill and Blake.

I have a dandy hutch

Without the rabbit.

If you see any such,

Will you please grab it?

David McCord

When asked how he came up with the idea for the story *Swimmy,* Leo Lionni said, "I was watching the minnows swimming around in the harbor one day. Standing by the water that day, I didn't have an idea for a book. But later, as I began writing the book, I realized seeing the fish gave me the idea and set the story off.

"For the art in this book, I used a lot of wet paint. To make the watery background, I put the paint on a piece of glass. Then I pressed paper onto the glass so it would pick up the paint. I used my hand to spread the paint. Then I lifted the paper off the glass, and it made a watery ocean for Swimmy and his friends. Then I cut up pieces of paper to make a collage. Swimmy and the little red fish were little rubber stamps."

Meet
Leo Lionni

CALDECOTT HONOR BOOK

immy

by _Leo Lionni_

A happy school of little fish
lived in a corner of the sea somewhere.
They were all red. Only one of them was
as black as a mussel shell. He swam
faster than his brothers and sisters. His
name was Swimmy.

One bad day a tuna fish, swift, fierce and very hungry, came darting through the waves. In one gulp he swallowed all the little red fish.

Only Swimmy escaped. He swam away in the deep wet world. He was scared, lonely and very sad.

But the sea was full of wonderful creatures, and as he swam from marvel to marvel Swimmy was happy again.

He saw a medusa made of rainbow jelly . . .

a lobster, who walked about like a
water-moving machine . . .

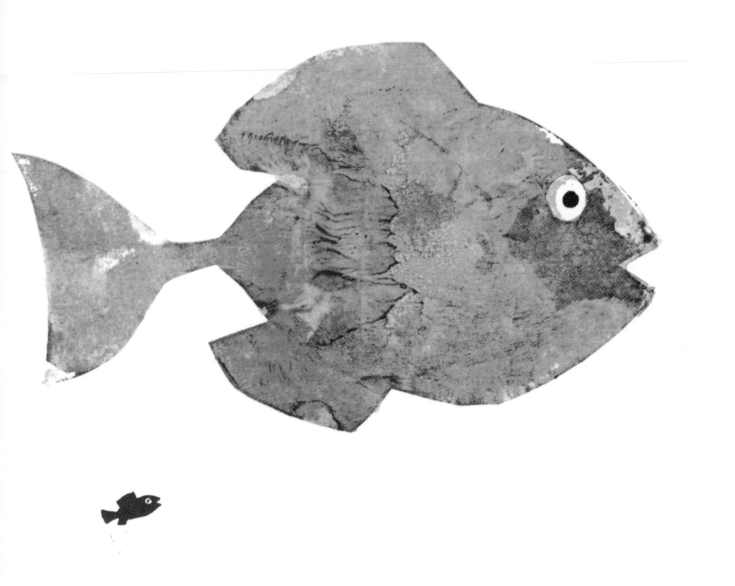

strange fish, pulled by an invisible thread . . .

335

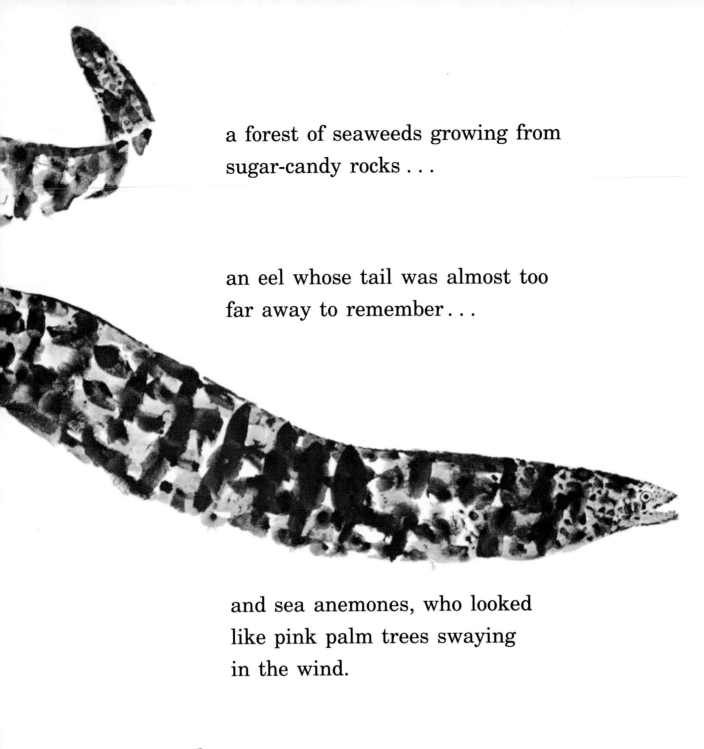

a forest of seaweeds growing from
sugar-candy rocks . . .

an eel whose tail was almost too
far away to remember . . .

and sea anemones, who looked
like pink palm trees swaying
in the wind.

Then, hidden in the dark shade of rocks and weeds, he saw a school of little fish, just like his own.

"Let's go and swim and play and SEE things!" he said happily.

"We can't," said the little red fish. "The big fish will eat us all."

"But you can't just lie there," said Swimmy. "We must THINK of something."

Swimmy thought and thought and thought. Then suddenly he said, "I have it! We are going to swim all together like the biggest fish in the sea!"

339

He taught them to swim close together, each in his own place, and when they had learned to swim like one giant fish, he said, "I'll be the eye."

And so they swam in the cool morning water and
in the midday sun and chased the big fish away.

THE LIGHT·HOUSE·KEEPER'S WHITE·MOUSE

by JOHN CIARDI

As I rowed out to the light-house
For a cup of tea one day,
I came on a very wet white-mouse
Out swimming in the bay.

"If you are for the light-house,"
Said he, "I'm glad we met.
I'm the light-house-keeper's white-mouse
And I fear I'm getting wet."

"O light-house-keeper's white-mouse,
I am rowing out for tea
With the keeper in his light-house.
Let me pull you in with me."

So I gave an oar to the white-mouse.
And I pulled on the other.
And we all had tea at the light-house
With the keeper and his mother.

343

Brochures

WELCOME TO THE
Aquarium

Dive right in! Discover marine life from the depths of the ocean to the surface of a backyard pond. Watch otters frolic and dolphins dance. And you won't want to miss our new Please Touch! exhibit—fun for children and adults of all ages!

ADMISSION
Adults	$5.00
Seniors and Students	$4.00
Children	$3.00
Children under 3	Free

HOURS
Sunday–Thursday:
10:00 A.M. to 5:00 P.M.
Friday and Saturday:
10:00 A.M. to 8:00 P.M.

WHAT'S GOING ON?

Daily Tours
See the Aquarium with our trained volunteer guides. Meet at the main entrance. Tours begin at 10:15, 11:15, 1:15, 2:15, 3:15.

Marine Life Films
Join us in the theater for exciting wildlife films. 1:00 and 3:00.

Feeding Times
Sea Lions 11:00, 2:00, 4:00
Penguins 10:30, 2:30

KEY
Restrooms

Telephone

Restaurant

Information

To Parking Area →

Wyeth Street

Gift Shop

Entrance

Brochures

Aquarium Guide

Picnic Area

Please Touch!

(Children's Exhibit)

Penguins

Eels

Rays

Theater

Sharks

Sea Lions

Sea Otters

Whales

Entrance

Ocean Avenue

Calendar
▼▼▼▼▼▼▼▼▼
1997

JANUARY

SUN	MON	TUES	WED	THURS	FRI	SAT
			1	2	3	4
5	6	7	8	9	10	11
12	13	14	15	16	17	18
19	20	21	22	23	24	25
26	27	28	29	30	31	

FEBRUARY

SUN	MON	TUES	WED	THURS	FRI	SAT
						1
2	3	4	5	6	7	8
9	10	11	12	13	14	15
16	17	18	19	20	21	22
23	24	25	26	27	28	

MARCH

SUN	MON	TUES	WED	THURS	FRI	SAT
						1
2	3	4	5	6	7	8
9	10	11	12	13	14	15
16	17	18	19	20	21	22
23/30	24/31	25	26	27	28	29

APRIL

SUN	MON	TUES	WED	THURS	FRI	SAT
		1	2	3	4	5
6	7	8	9	10	11	12
13	14	15	16	17	18	19
20	21	22	23	24	25	26
27	28	29	30			

MAY

SUN	MON	TUES	WED	THURS	FRI	SAT
				1	2	3
4	5	6	7	8	9	10
11	12	13	14	15	16	17
18	19	20	21	22	23	24
25	26	27	28	29	30	31

JUNE

SUN	MON	TUES	WED	THURS	FRI	SAT
1	2	3	4	5	6	7
8	9	10	11	12	13	14
15	16	17	18	19	20	21
22	23	24	25	26	27	28
29	30					

JULY

SUN	MON	TUES	WED	THURS	FRI	SAT
		1	2	3	4	5
6	7	8	9	10	11	12
13	14	15	16	17	18	19
20	21	22	23	24	25	26
27	28	29	30	31		

AUGUST

SUN	MON	TUES	WED	THURS	FRI	SAT
					1	2
3	4	5	6	7	8	9
10	11	12	13	14	15	16
17	18	19	20	21	22	23
24/31	25	26	27	28	29	30

SEPTEMBER

SUN	MON	TUES	WED	THURS	FRI	SAT
	1	2	3	4	5	6
7	8	9	10	11	12	13
14	15	16	17	18	19	20
21	22	23	24	25	26	27
28	29	30				

OCTOBER

SUN	MON	TUES	WED	THURS	FRI	SAT
			1	2	3	4
5	6	7	8	9	10	11
12	13	14	15	16	17	18
19	20	21	22	23	24	25
26	27	28	29	30	31	

NOVEMBER

SUN	MON	TUES	WED	THURS	FRI	SAT
						1
2	3	4	5	6	7	8
9	10	11	12	13	14	15
16	17	18	19	20	21	22
23/30	24	25	26	27	28	29

DECEMBER

SUN	MON	TUES	WED	THURS	FRI	SAT
	1	2	3	4	5	6
7	8	9	10	11	12	13
14	15	16	17	18	19	20
21	22	23	24	25	26	27
28	29	30	31			

PRESIDENT'S DAY!
FEBRUARY 17th

Directions
▼▼▼▼▼▼▼▼

NATURAL DYEING

WHAT YOU WILL NEED:

- stove or hot plate
- large kettle
- water
- a white cotton garment (T-shirt, socks)
- various natural substances

NATURAL SUBSTANCES DYE CHART

marigold flowers		red onion skin	
sage		acorns	
walnut shells		berries	
tea		coffee	
spinach		dandelion roots	
yellow onion skin		beets	

Directions

WHAT TO DO:

1. **Fill the large kettle with water and put it on the stove or hot plate.**

2. **Turn on the heat.**

3. **Add the natural substance for the color you want.**

4. **Allow the water to simmer until it is darker than you want your garment to be.**

5. **Put the garment loosely into the water and simmer it until it is darker than you want it. (The garment will be lighter when it dries.)**

6. **Remove the garment from the kettle and rinse it in cold water.**

7. **Wring out the garment and hang it up to dry.**

8. **If you are not going to dye anything else, turn off the heat and empty the kettle.**

Maps

NEW JERSEY

THE BRONX

HUDSON RIVER

MANHATTAN

QUEENS

■ 1.
■ 2.

GOVERNOR'S ISLAND

■ 3.
Buttermilk
Channel

Red Hook

BROOKLYN

UPPER
NEW YORK
BAY

The
Narrows

STATEN
ISLAND

VERRAZANO-
NARROWS
BRIDGE

LOWER
NEW YORK
BAY

A T L A N

Maps

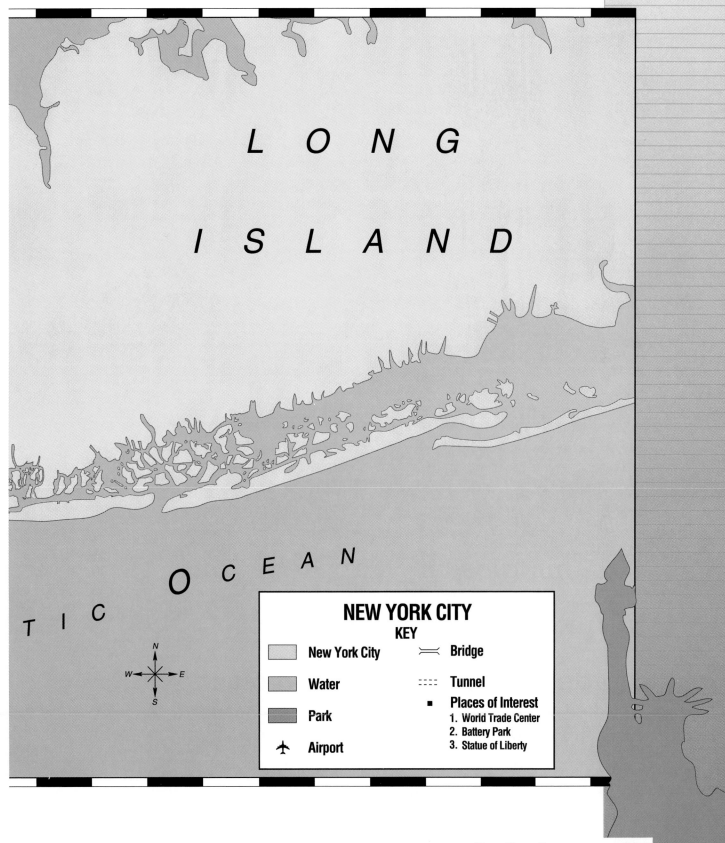

LONG ISLAND

ATLANTIC OCEAN

NEW YORK CITY
KEY

New York City

Water

Park

✈ Airport

⟩⟨ Bridge

---- Tunnel

■ Places of Interest
1. World Trade Center
2. Battery Park
3. Statue of Liberty

N
W E
S

GLOS

This glossary can help you
to find out the meanings of
words in this book that you may
not know.

SARY

The words are listed in
alphabetical order. Guide words
at the top of each page tell you the
first and last words on the page.

Aa

airplane

An **airplane** is a large vehicle that can fly. An **airplane** can carry people, packages, and other things from one place to another. ▲ **airplanes.**

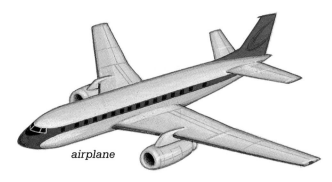
airplane

almost

Almost means close to. It is **almost** 2 o'clock.

angry

When people are **angry** they are mad at someone or something. Mom was **angry** at the dog for chewing her slippers. ▲ **angrier, angriest.**

answer

An **answer** is the solution to a problem. Sue knew the **answer** to the math problem. ▲ **answered, answering.**

apartment

An **apartment** is a set of rooms to live in found in a large building. Sam lives in an **apartment** with his family. ▲ **apartments.**

asleep

When you are **asleep,** you are not awake. Nina had a funny dream while she was **asleep.**

asleep

awful

Awful means terrible or very bad. The medicine I had to take tasted **awful.**

Bb

beat

Beat means to hit something again and again. The rain **beat** against the window. ▲ **beaten, beating.**

become

To **become** means to grow to be something. Kittens grow older and **become** cats. ▲ **became, becoming.**

bedroom

A **bedroom** is a room that people use for sleeping. The sun came through my **bedroom** window. ▲ **bedrooms.**

between

Between means in the middle of two other things. In the alphabet, *s* comes **between** *r* and *t*.

beyond

Beyond means on the far side of. Our camp is just **beyond** those trees.

bottom

The **bottom** is the lowest part of something. The rock sank to the **bottom** of the pool. ▲ **bottoms.**

breath

Breath is the air you take in and let out when you breathe. When it is very cold, you can see your **breath.** ▲ **breaths.**

bridge

A **bridge** is something that is built across water. We drove over the **bridge.** ▲ **bridges.**

bridge

brush

Brush means to clean or make something neat using a light stroking movement. Jim likes to **brush** his dog at least once a week. ▲ **brushed, brushing.**

build

To **build** means to make something. They wanted to **build** a sandcastle at the beach. ▲ **built, building, builds.**

build

busy

When people are **busy,** they are doing something. Roberta can't come out to play because she is **busy** doing her homework. ▲ **busier, busiest.**

Cc

careful

If you are **careful,** you are thinking about what you are doing. Tina is very **careful** not to spill the paint.

carry

Carry means to hold something while moving it from one place to another. Mike will **carry** the groceries into the house for his mom. ▲ **carried, carrying.**

choose

Choose means to pick out something you want to have. Billy wanted to **choose** a gift for his grandmother. ▲ **chose, chosen, choosing.**

corner

A **corner** is a place where two lines or sides come together. Paul bumped his knee on the **corner** of the table. ▲ **corners.**

course

When you follow a **course**, you follow a certain way to get from one place to another. The airplane flew off its **course** because of the storm. ▲ **courses.**

curly

Curly means that something is in the shape of a little circle. Sally has **curly** hair. ▲ **curlier, curliest.**

decide

When you **decide** to do something, you choose to do one thing instead of another. Carlos may **decide** to have cereal instead of eggs. ▲ **decided, deciding.**

different

When something is **different**, it is not the same as something else. A duck is **different** from a goose.

different

G5

downstairs

When you go **downstairs,** you go to a lower floor. I went **downstairs** to answer the door.

dream

A **dream** is a picture in your mind that you have when you are asleep. Last night Carol had a **dream** that she could fly.
▲ **dreams.**

duplicate

Duplicate means to make an exact copy of something or to do something again. We tried to **duplicate** last year's victory.
▲ **duplicated, duplicating.**

dye

To **dye** means to color or stain cloth, hair, food, or other materials. Robin's cousin wanted to **dye** his hair red. Another word that sounds like this is **die.** ▲ **dyes, dyeing.**

Ee

Earth

Earth is the planet we live on. It takes one year for **Earth** to go around the sun.

Earth

easy

When something is **easy,** it is not hard to do. The test was **easy.** ▲ **easier, easiest.**

either

Either is used when we talk about two of anything, and we mean one or the other. Rosie wanted **either** a ball or a kite.

escape

Escape means to get away from something. People knew that a hurricane was coming and were able to **escape** without getting hurt.
▲ **escaped, escaping.**

explain

When you **explain** something, you help another person understand it. Rosa will **explain** her poem to the class.
▲ **explained, explaining.**

finish

Finish means to get to the end of something. When I **finish** writing the letter, I will mail it.
▲ **finished, finishing.**

flop

To move around or flap loosely. The dog's ears **flop** when it runs.
▲ **flopped, flopping.**

forest

A **forest** is a large area of land covered by trees and other plants. They went camping in the **forest.**
▲ **forests.**

forest

forever

Forever means something that will never end. The boy and girl in the fairy tale wanted to stay young **forever.**

forget

Forget means to not remember something. Josie was afraid she would **forget** my address, so she wrote it down. ▲ **forgot, forgetting.**

Gg

garden

A **garden** is a place where people grow flowers or vegetables. When our cousins visit, they always bring us fresh tomatoes from their **garden.** ▲ **gardens.**

garden

giant

1. Giant means very big. Many of the dinosaurs that lived millions of years ago were **giant** animals.
2. A **giant** is also a huge make-believe person. The **giant** in the story could hold three people in one hand. ▲ **giants.**

giant

giggle

When you **giggle** you laugh in a silly way. We began to **giggle** when my little brother put his socks on his ears. ▲ **giggled, giggling.**

grab

Grab means to take hold of suddenly. The baby tried to **grab** my hair. ▲ **grabbed, grabbing.**

grandmother

Your **grandmother** is your father's mother or your mother's mother. Sometimes a **grandmother** is called grandma or nana. My **grandmother** lives in New York City. ▲ **grandmothers.**

growl

Growl means to make a deep, angry sound in the throat. The dogs **growl** when someone knocks on the door. ▲ **growled, growling.**

happen

Happen means to take place. If you listen to the story, you will hear what **happens** next. ▲ **happened, happening.**

harbor

A **harbor** is a safe place for boats near the shore in either lakes, rivers, or oceans. We watched the fishing boats come into the **harbor.** ▲ **harbors.**

harbor

hide

Hide means to put yourself or something else in a place where it cannot be seen. My cat likes to **hide** under my bed. ▲ **hid, hidden,** or **hid, hiding.**

G9

Ii

important

When something is **important,** it means that you should pay attention to it. It is **important** that you look both ways before you cross the street.

island

An **island** is land that has water all around it. My aunt lives on an **island,** so we have to take a boat to visit her. ▲ **islands.**

Kk

kitchen

A **kitchen** is a room where people cook and serve food. Martin's family eats in the **kitchen.** ▲ **kitchens.**

Ll

large

Large means big. Elephants and whales are **large** animals. ▲ **larger, largest.**

lei

A **lei** is a chain made of flowers often worn in Hawaii. When Kate went to visit her aunt in Hawaii she was given a beautiful **lei**. Another word that sounds like this is **lay**. ▲ **leis.**

lei

linen

Linen is a strong cloth made from the flax plant used to make clothing, tablecloths, and sheets. My aunt was busy folding the **linen** napkins.

lonely

1. When you feel **lonely,** you feel unhappy about being by yourself. Gabe is **lonely** because all his friends are away for the summer. **2.** Something that is away from others. A **lonely** tree grew in the field. ▲ **lonelier, loneliest.**

loud

Something that is **loud** makes a lot of noise. The alarm clock made a **loud** buzzing noise. ▲ **louder, loudest.**

Mm

middle

The **middle** is a place halfway between two points or sides. Noon is in the **middle** of the day. ▲ **middles.**

Nn

nature

Nature means all things in the world that are not made by people. Plants, animals, mountains, and oceans are all part of **nature.**

notice

1. When you **notice** something, you see it or pay attention to it. In the autumn, Erin began to **notice** that the days seemed to be getting shorter and the nights seemed to be getting longer. ▲ **noticed, noticing.**

2. A **notice** also means a printed message to make something known. Benji got a **notice** that the circus was coming to town next week. ▲ **notices.**

Oo

ocean

An **ocean** is a body of salt water and covers large areas of the earth. Fish and whales live in the ocean. ▲ **oceans.**

often

When something happens **often** it happens many times over and over again. Kate **often** eats cereal for breakfast.

Pp

pajamas

Pajamas are a shirt and a pair of pants that you wear when you go to bed. Jessica's favorite **pajamas** have red polka dots.

planet

A **planet** is any one of the nine large bodies that revolve around the sun, including Earth. The spaceship landed on the **planet** Mars. ▲ **planets.**

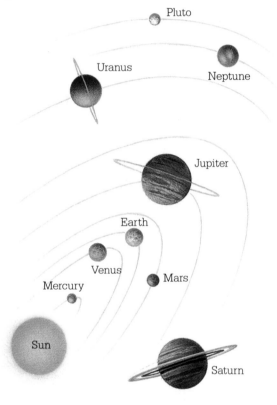

Pluto

Uranus

Neptune

Jupiter

Earth

Venus

Mars

Mercury

Sun

Saturn

planet

practice

Practice means doing something over and over until you do it well. I will **practice** riding my bike after school. ▲ **practiced, practicing.**

G12

pretend

Pretend means to make believe. Tomás and Janie often **pretend** to be robots. ▲ **pretended, pretending.**

pull

When you **pull** something, you move it toward you. I tried to **pull** the door open. ▲ **pulled, pulling.**

purr

Purr means to make a soft, quiet sound. Cats **purr** when they are happy. ▲ **purred, purring.**

Qq

quick

When something is **quick,** it means that it moves fast or happens in a short time. We ate a **quick** lunch. ▲ **quicker, quickest.**

quilt

A **quilt** is like a blanket. I sleep under a soft, warm **quilt** during the winter. ▲ **quilts.**

Rr

rainbow

The bright colors you sometimes see in the sky after it rains are called a **rainbow.** The **rainbow** appeared after the thunderstorm. ▲ **rainbows.**

rainbow

rattle

To **rattle** means to make a lot of short, sharp sounds by shaking or hitting something. The windows **rattle** when the wind blows during a storm.
▲ **rattled, rattling.**

rush

Rush means to move, go, or come quickly. We have to **rush** or we'll miss the bus and be late for school.
▲ **rushed, rushing.**

Ss

safe

Safe means to be protected from danger. William put his favorite book on the shelf where it would be **safe**. ▲ **safer, safest.**

scare

If something **scares** you, it makes you feel afraid. Loud noises always **scare** the puppy. ▲ **scared, scaring.**

shell

A **shell** is a hard outer covering that protects something. A turtle has a hard **shell** on its back.
▲ **shells.**

shell

shine

Shine means to give out light or to be bright. The sun **shines** during the day.
▲ **shone** or **shined, shining.**

short

Short means not far from one end to another. My dog has **short** legs. ▲ **shorter, shortest.**

signal

To **signal** is to show people what to do without using words. The children waited for the crossing guard to **signal** them to cross the street. ▲ **signals.**

signal

smart

A person who is **smart** is clever or bright. Leah is a **smart** girl who does well in school. ▲ **smarter, smartest.**

soft

When a sound is **soft,** it is gentle and quiet. Since the baby was sleeping, the mother spoke in a very **soft** voice.

space

1. Space is a place that has nothing in it. Write your name in the **space** on the paper. ▲ **spaces.**
2. Space is also the place where all of the planets and stars are found. The earth, moon, and sun are in **space.**

spin

Spin means to go around in a circle. Chuck loves to **spin** his toy top. ▲ **spun, spinning.**

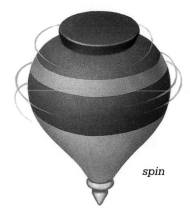

spin

G15

storm

During a **storm,** it rains or snows and the wind blows hard. I wore my raincoat during the **storm.** ▲ **storms.**

storm

straight

If something is **straight,** it does not bend. I used a ruler to draw a **straight** line on the paper.

▲ **straighter, straightest.**

stripe

A **stripe** is a long line that is a different color from what is next to it. Sally wore a blue shirt with a green **stripe** to the party. ▲ **stripes.**

strong

If something is **strong,** it means that it has a lot of power. The wind was so **strong** that it blew down a big tree. ▲ **stronger, strongest.**

sudden

When something is **sudden,** it means it happens very fast. There was a **sudden** storm. ▲ **suddenly.**

sunlight

Sunlight is the light from the sun. Plants, animals, and humans all need **sunlight** to grow and to be healthy.

Tt

through

1. **Through** means from one side or end to the other. The children crawled **through** the tunnel in the playground.
2. **Through** also means finished. I will be **through** with my homework soon.

treasure

A **treasure** is money, jewelry, or other things that are of great value. The king and queen hid their **treasure** in a special room. ▲ **treasures.**

treasure

twig

A **twig** is a tiny branch of a tree. After climbing the tree, I found a **twig** in my hair. ▲ **twigs.**

Uu

upstairs

When you go **upstairs,** you go to a higher floor. My brother's bedroom is downstairs, but my bedroom is **upstairs.**

Ww

whale

A **whale** is a very large animal that lives in the ocean. I saw a blue **whale** at the aquarium.
▲ **whales.**

wild

To be **wild** means that something is not controlled by people and lives naturally. There are **wild** horses living on that island. ▲ **wilder, wildest.**

wonderful

Wonderful means amazing, unusual, or very good. At the circus we all stared at the **wonderful** acrobats.

wool

Wool is a kind of cloth that is made from the hair of a sheep or other animals. **Wool** is used to make sweaters, mittens, coats, and blankets.

wool

worry

When you **worry** it means that you feel a little afraid about something. Mom and Dad start to **worry** if we come home late from school. ▲ **worried, worrying.**

wrap

Wrap means to cover something by putting something else around it. We will **wrap** a blanket around us to keep warm. ▲ **wrapped, wrapping.**

yarn

Yarn is thread spun from fiber that has been twisted into long strands. Amy's grandmother is making each of her grandchildren a sweater out of **yarn.**

ACKNOWLEDGMENTS

The publisher gratefully acknowledges permission to reprint the following copyrighted material:

"Adopting Daisy," art by Mike Eagle, from LADYBUG, THE MAGAZINE FOR YOUNG CHILDREN, October 1993 issue, Copyright © 1993, Carus Publishing Company. Reprinted by permission.

"Andre" by Gwendolyn Brooks. Reprinted by permission.

Cover illustration of CAN I KEEP HIM? by Steven Kellogg. Copyright © 1971 by Steven Kellogg. Used by permission of Dial Books for Young Readers, a division of Penguin Books USA Inc.

"Carry Go Bring Come." From CARRY GO BRING COME by Vyanne Samuels. Copyright © 1988 by Jennifer Northway. Reprinted with the permission of Simon & Schuster Books For Young Children. Reprinted also by permission of the Bodley Head.

"Charlie Anderson" by Barbara Abercrombie, illustrated by Mark Graham, Text copyright © 1990 by Barbara Abercrombie, Illustrations copyright © 1990 by Mark Graham, published by Simon and Schuster. Reprinted by permission.

"Everybody Says" by Dorothy Aldis reprinted by permission of G.P. Putnam & Sons from EVERYTHING AND ANYTHING, copyright © 1925-1927, © renewed 1953-1955 by Dorothy Aldis.

The book cover of FLY AWAY HOME by Eve Bunting, illustrated by Ronald Himler. Copyright © 1991, published by Clarion Books of Houghton Mifflin, is reprinted by permission of the publisher.

"The Goat in the Rug" from THE GOAT IN THE RUG by Charles Blood and Martin A. Link. Copyright © 1980 by Charles L. Blood and Martin A. Link. Illustrations copyright © 1980 by Nancy Winslow Parker. Reprinted with the permission of Simon & Schuster Books For Young Readers.

The book cover of HENRY AND MUDGE AND THE FOREVER SEA by Cynthia Rylant, illustrated by Suçie Stevenson. Reprinted with the permission of Simon & Schuster Books For Young Readers.

"Henry and Mudge: The First Book" reprinted with the permission of Simon & Schuster Books For Young Readers from HENRY AND MUDGE: THE FIRST BOOK by Cynthia Rylant, illustrated by Suçie Stevenson. Text, copyright © 1987 by Cynthia Rylant. Illustrations copyright © 1987 by Suçie Stevenson.

"Henry's Wrong Turn" from HENRY'S WRONG TURN by Harriet Ziefert. Text Copyright © 1989 by Harriet Ziefert; Illustrations Copyright © 1989 by Andrea Baruffi. By permission of Little, Brown and Company.

"Hey, Bug!" by Lilian Moore. Reprinted by permission.

"Hugs and Kisses" from THE SUN IS ON by Lindamichellebaron. Reprinted by permission of Harlin Jacque Publications.

Cover from THE ISLAND OF THE SKOG by Steven Kellogg. Copyright © 1973 by Steven Kellogg. Used by permission of Dial Books for Young Readers, a division of Penguin Books USA Inc.

"Lei Day: Party in the Islands!" reprinted from OWL magazine with permission of the publisher, Owl Communications Inc., Toronto, Canada.

"The Light-House-Keeper's White-Mouse" from YOU READ TO ME, I'LL READ TO YOU by John Ciardi. Copyright © 1962 by John Ciardi. Copyright © 1990 renewed. Reprinted by permission of Mrs. Judith Ciardi.

"Looking Around" by Aileen Fisher. Reprinted by permission.

"Lost" from FAR AND FEW by David McCord. Copyright by David McCord © 1952 by David McCord. By permission Little, Brown and Company.

"Luka's Quilt" by Georgia Guback. Copyright © 1994 by Georgia Guback, published by Greenwillow Books. Reprinted by permission.

"My Horse, Fly Like a Bird" Copyright © 1989 by Virginia Driving Hawk Sneve. All rights reserved. Reprinted from DANCING TEPEES: POEMS OF AMERICAN INDIAN YOUTH by permission of Holiday House.

"The Mysterious Tadpole" from THE MYSTERIOUS TADPOLE by Steven Kellogg. Copyright © by Steven Kellogg. Used by permission of Dial Books for Young Readers, a division of Penguin Books USA Inc.

"Nine-in-One, Grr! Grr!" by Blia Xiong reprinted with permission of Children's Book Press, San Francisco, CA.

"October Saturday" by Bobbie Katz. Copyright © 1990 by Bobbie Katz. Used by permission of Bobbie Katz, who controls all rights.

The book cover of PATRICK'S DINOSAURS by Carol Carrick, illustrated by Donald Carrick, Copyright © 1983, published by Clarion Books of Houghton Mifflin, is reprinted by permission of the publisher.

"The Puppy and I" from WHEN WE WERE VERY YOUNG by A. A. Milne. Illustrations by E. H. Shepard. Copyright © 1924 by E. P. Dutton, renewed 1952 by A. A. Milne. Used by permission of Dutton's Children's Books, a division of Penguin Books USA Inc.

"Relatives" from THE BUTTERFLY JAR by Jeff Moss. Used by permission of Bantam Books, a division of Bantam Doubleday Dell Publishing Group, Inc.

The book cover of SLEEP OUT by Carol Carrick, illustrated by Donald Carrick. Copyright © 1979, published by Clarion Books of Houghton Mifflin, is reprinted by permission of the publisher.

"A Spike of Green" by Barbara Baker. Reprinted by permission.

"The Sun Is Always Shining Somewhere" by Allan Fowler, Copyright © 1991 by Children's Press, Inc., published by Children's Press. Reprinted by permission.

"Swimmy" from SWIMMY by Leo Lionni. Copyright © 1963 by Leo Lionni. Reprinted by permission of Pantheon Books, a division of Random House, Inc.

"Tigers" from YOUR BIG BACKYARD Series 1, Number 5, May 1995 issue, copyright © 1980, published by the National Wildlife Federation. Reprinted by permission.

The book cover of THE WALL by Eve Bunting, illustrated by Ronald Himler, Copyright © 1990, published by Houghton Mifflin, is reprinted by permission of the publisher.

"The Wednesday Surprise" from THE WEDNESDAY SURPRISE by Eve Bunting with illustrations by Donald Carrick. Text copyright © 1989 by Eve Bunting. Illustrations copyright © 1989 by Donald Carrick. Reprinted by permission of Clarion Books, a Houghton Mifflin Co. imprint.

"What in the World?" from THERE IS NO RHYME FOR SILVER by Eve Merriam. Copyright © 1962 by Eve Merriam. Copyright renewed by Eve Merriam. Reprinted by permission of Marian Reiner for author.

"What Is a Shadow?" by Bob Ridiman, Art by True Kelley, from LADYBUG magazine for young children July 1993 issue, copyright © 1993, published by Carus Publishing Company. Reprinted by permission.

"Willie's Not the Hugging Kind" is the entire work from WILLIE'S NOT THE HUGGING KIND by Joyce Durham Barrett, illustrated by Pat Cummings. Text copyright © 1989 by Joyce Durham Barrett. Illustrations copyright © 1989 by Pat Cummings. Reprinted by permission of Harper/Collins Publishers.

"A Wool Surprise for Kenji" by Sue Katharine Jackson, illustrated by Dora Leder, from LADYBUG magazine for young children January 1994 issue, Copyright © 1994, published by Carus Publishing Company. Reprinted by permission.

READING RESOURCES

Book Parts: Excerpt from HENRY AND MUDGE AND THE BEDTIME THUMPS by Cynthia Rylant, illustrated by Suçie Stevenson. Text, copyright © 1991 by Cynthia Rylant. Illustration, copyright © by Suçie Stevenson. Reprinted by permission of Simon & Schuster Books For Young Children.

Dictionary: Excerpt from MACMILLAN PRIMARY DICTIONARY. copyright © 1991 by Macmillan/McGraw-Hill School Publishing Company. Reprinted by permission of Macmillan/McGraw-Hill School Publishing Company.

COVER DESIGN: Carbone Smolan Associates
COVER ILLUSTRATION: Floyd Cooper

DESIGN CREDITS
Carbone Smolan Associates, front matter, 234-235
Bill Smith Studio, 292-295
Function Thru Form, Inc., 344-347
Notovitz Design Inc., 348-351

ILLUSTRATION CREDITS
Floyd Cooper, 234-235; Carol Schwartz, 236-237; Margaret Cusack, 292 (title); Krista Brauckmann-Towns, 298-299; John Steven Gurney, 324-325; Loretta Krupinski, 342-343. **Reading Resources:** Bob Mansfield, 344-345; Alex Bloch, 348-349; Graphic Chart and Map Co., 350-351. **Glossary:** Will and Cory Nelson, G2, G5, G8, G10, G12, G14, G15, G17; Bob Pepper, G4.

PHOTOGRAPHY CREDITS
All photographs are by the Macmillan/McGraw-Hill School Division (MMSD) except as noted below.

265: b. Michael Biondo. 290: m. courtesy Martin Link; b. courtesy Charles L. Blood. 291: Jay Carpenter. 296-297: F. Dennis Lessard, courtesy of Chandler Institute, Santa Fe, New Mexico. 321: b. Courtesy Andrea Baruffi. 326: r. Massimi Pacifico, courtesy of Knopf. 346: Monica Stevenson for MMSD. 347: Charles Thatcher/Tony Stone Images. **Glossary:** G0: Inga Spence/Tom Stack & Associates; Superstock; Comstock. G1: Jack Van Antwerp/The Stock Market; Craig Tuttle/The Stock Market; Richard Gross/The Stock Market. G2: b.r. Bob Daemmrich/Stock Boston. G3: b.r. Thomas Kitchin/Tom Stock & Associates. G6: m. Tony Stone Images. G7: m. Doug Sokell/Tom Stack & Associates. G8: b.l. Bill Ross/Westlight. G9: W. Cody/Westlight. G13: David Olsen/Tony Stone Images. G15: b.l. Robert Daemmrich/Tony Stone Images. G16: l. Renee Purre/Photo Researchers, Inc. G18: b. Gale Zucker/Stock Boston.